THE LITTLE BOOK OF

GW00631100

summersdale

Summersdale Publishers Ltd
46 West Street
Chichester
West Sussex
PO19 1RP
United Kingdom

www.summersdale.com

ISBN 1 84024 372 4

Printed in Great Britain.

IMPORTANT WARNING:
DRINKING EXCESS ALCOHOL CAN DAMAGE YOUR HEALTH.

The publisher urges care and caution in the pursuit of any practices related to the activities represented in this book. **This book is intended for use by adults only.** The publisher cannot accept any responsibility for the result of the use or misuse of this book or any loss, injury or damage caused thereby.

Contents

Introduction

Most of these games have one thing in common: they combine a full glass with making a fool of yourself – all the ingredients for a great night, in fact.

These games all take different formats (cards, luck, word association, etc) but the outcome is always the same . . . the players are left laughing at each other.

So gather your friends and crack open your favourite poison: here's a whole collection of ways to demonstrate your mental skills and dexterity and humiliate yourself in the grand name of fun.

The 2-Finger Rule

Whenever you are instructed to drink in this book, you are expected to do so with moderation. To make things fair, it is best to decide on a set measurement for your drinking penalty. A good version is the '2-finger rule', but you can agree upon another amount between yourselves.

Drink This Much!

Strength Rating –

Can You Handle It?

 – Merry Jerry

 – Lairy Mary

 – Sloshed Josh

You Will Need:

Some friends . . .

. . . and some drink

NB. Ensure that you gather the appropriate type of people.

If you're not Up For It,
you shouldn't be reading this book!

The Games

Musical Chairs

Strength Rating –

You will need:

 drink

 friends

 chairs

 music

Arrange the chairs in a circle facing outwards, making sure there is one chair less than the number of players.

One person acts as the DJ and plays some music while the players walk around the chairs with their drinks in their hands. When the music stops they must all try to sit down. Whoever fails to get a seat must have some of their drink, and is out of the game. Whoever spills their drink in the scramble must also drink, but they continue in the game.

Remove a chair and repeat the game, losing one person and one chair in each round until there is an eventual winner.

The Magic Roundabout

Strength Rating –

You will need:

 drink

 friends

 a pack of cards

Spread the cards out in a circle, to form the 'roundabout'. One player picks a card. Then the person next to them picks a card.

14

If the cards are of the same suit, add up the values of the two cards and the two people have to take that number of gulps of their drink.

If they aren't the same then the first person puts their card in a discard pile and the next person draws a card. If it matches the second person's suit then they drink a number of gulps equal to the combined value of the two cards. If you get three cards of the same suit in a row, or even four, add up to total value and drink that number.

Mallet's Mallet

Strength Rating – 🍺 🍺 🍺

You will need:

 drink

 friends

 a pack of cards

Discard all cards from 2 to 9 (inclusive). Place a full glass of drink in the middle of the table, and spread the 20 remaining cards face down, around the glass. Take it in turns to draw a card, performing the following actions according to the card drawn:

16

10 =   'Mallet's Mallet' . . . play a quick round of word association (one word each, must be related to the previous word, hesitation or irrelevance is punished by drinking).

Jack =   Social drink – every player has to have a drink.

Queen = Everyone drinks.

King =   That player nominates one person to drink.

Ace =   Nothing happens when the first three Aces are drawn, but whoever draws the final Ace must drink the entire glass on the table.

The Peanut Race

Strength Rating –

You will need:

 drink

 friends

 a bag of salted peanuts

The idea is for each player to drop a peanut into their own full glass at exactly the same time when someone shouts 'Drop!' The peanut will sink to the bottom, then rise up again.

The player whose peanut comes to the surface last is the loser, and must drink their entire glass. The loser's glass is then refilled and another round is played. After a round each player must retrieve the peanut from their glass, eat it, and choose a new one.

The Personality Game

Strength Rating –

You will need:

 drink

 friends

Sit around a table. The first person turns to the person on their right and says the name of a famous person. The next person has to think of a personality whose name begins with the first letter of the previous famous person's surname, e.g. if the first celebrity named is Bill Clinton, the next

20

one could be Carrie Fisher, and the
next could be Fred Astaire, and so on.
This continues around the table and will
only reverse directions if someone says
a name where the first letter of the first
name and the first letter of the surname
are the same, such as Boris Becker.

The most important rule is that you
must play this game without pausing. If
you do pause you have to 'Drink While
You Think!' – continuous drinking until
you think of a person.

Who Am I?

Strength Rating –

You will need:

 drink

 friends

 a pen and paper

 some sticky tape

One player writes down the name of a famous person on a piece of paper and sticks it to the forehead of another player. Everyone can see the name on the paper except the person on whose forehead it is stuck. This person must find out who they are by asking questions to each player in turn. Only 'yes' or 'no' may be given as answers. For every 'no' given the person asking the questions must have some of their drink.

The James Bond Game

Strength Rating –

You will need:

 drink

 friends

 a James Bond film

You must have a drink whenever one of the following occurs:

- someone says 'James'
- someone says 'Bond'
- Bond gets a new gadget
- Bond wears a dinner suit
- Bond seduces a woman
- Someone attempts to kill Bond
- Bond gets told off by M or Q
- a Bond girl wears a bikini
- Bond drinks a vodka martini
- Felix appears
- there is a car chase
- Bond makes a cheesy pun
- something explodes
- Bond breaks a new gadget
- the Bond theme is played

Sentence

Strength Rating –

You will need:

 drink

 friends

Someone starts with a word, any word. The next person has to say a word that could make a sentence with the word that has just been said, and so on.

The game goes on until someone says a word that doesn't make sense, or until someone hesitates, or until they laugh so much that they can't talk. This person then has to have a drink and the game continues.

The sentences constructed when this game is played can become absolutely bizarre, especially if some of the players are lateral thinkers, but as long as the sentence makes grammatical sense it will count.

Party Snap

Strength Rating –

You will need:

 drink

 friends

 a pack of cards

The more players, the better. Nominate one person to be the dealer. This role changes with each round because the dealer doesn't get to play that round. The dealer begins by placing cards, face up, in a stack, and calls out the number on each turn.

When two cards of the same number come up in sequence, the first person to bring their hand down onto the top of the pile and shout 'Snap!' gets the top card, and is then allowed to nominate a player to drink a number of gulps of their drink equal to the number of the card. A round ends when the dealer has no more cards.

Name That Tune

Strength Rating –

You will need:

 drink

 friends

 a CD player

One person is the DJ, and the others take turns to identify songs within their first five seconds. If a song is incorrectly guessed, the player must have some of their drink. A player can choose to

30

attempt identification in less than five seconds, subject to the following drinking penalties if they get it wrong:

A wrong guess at 4 seconds = 2 gulps

A wrong guess at 3 seconds = 3 gulps

A wrong guess at 2 seconds = 4 gulps

A wrong guess at 1 second = the entire drink

Just A Minute

Strength Rating –

You will need:

 drink

 friends

 a watch

The object of the game is to talk for 60 seconds on a subject without repetition, hesitation or deviation. One player acts as Judge, with responsibility for nominating a subject and keeping time.

Another player starts talking about the subject. If they hesitate, deviate or repeat themself another player can interrupt. If the interruption is considered valid by the Judge, a drinking penalty is handed out, and the person who interrupted gets to continue talking on the subject for the remainder of the minute.

Each change of speaker results in drinking a specified amount by the outgoing speaker. Whoever is speaking when the minute is up gets to nominate a person to drink, and becomes the judge in the next game.

Fuzzy Duck

Strength Rating –

You will need:

 drink

 friends

The first person in the row turns to their left and says, 'Fuzzy Duck'. The next person turns to their left and does the same. This continues until somebody turns to the person who's just said 'Fuzzy Duck' to them, and says 'Duzzy?' The question 'Duzzy?' can only be asked

34

twice by the same person per round. The question changes the direction and the phrase changes to 'Ducky Fuzz'. Anyone can reverse the direction by saying 'Duzzy?' The idea is to go round as fast as you can. Stalling or getting it wrong means you have to have a drink.

It's probably best not to play this one within earshot of your mother-in-law/ local priest/young children; the game can result in some very rude words being thrown about!

Slap, Clap, Click

Strength Rating –

You will need:

 drink

 friends

This is one of the hardest games to play . . . those without a sense of rhythm will be in trouble!

Before starting the game a category has to be decided. Players sit in a circle or around a table and begin the game by slapping their thighs with both hands, then clapping their hands together and finally clicking their fingers twice. This routine should build up into a steady 4-beat rhythm.

Whilst the players are doing this they have to take turns to call out a word belonging to the category decided, keeping strictly to the rhythm. If a player fails to think of a word when the beat gets to them, they must have a drink. If anyone loses rhythm or says a word that doesn't fit the category, they must have a drink.

One Big Chicken

Strength Rating –

You will need:

 drink

 8 people

Play the game person by person. Each person takes a phrase but the sixth person has to repeat the sixth phrase as well as the other five phrases. If they get the phrases wrong they have to gulp their drink to the number of phrases they should have said and then

38

start with the first phrase again. This carries on until all eight phrases are said without making a single mistake.

Phrases:

- Big chicken
- Sweet ducks
- Furry running rabbits
- Large ladies, sitting, sipping cider, and smoking cigarettes
- Sheets slit by Sam the sheet slitter
- Saucy Siamese sailors sailing the seven seas
- Echoing egoists echoing egotistical ecstasies
- Fig pluckers plucking figs, I'm not a fig plucker or a fig plucker's son but I'll pluck figs until the fig plucking's done!

Kings and Blood

Strength Rating –

You will need:

 drink

 friends

 a pack of cards

Shuffle a pack of cards, then spread them out on a table, face down. Put an empty glass in the middle of the table. Go around the table drawing the cards, one at a time.

If you draw a red card, have a drink. If you draw a black card, don't drink.

Whenever you draw one of the Kings, pour some drink into the glass in the centre of the table (the quantity is up to the player). Whoever draws the final (fourth) King, must drink the centre glass.

The Dictator Game

Strength Rating –

You will need:

 drink

 friends

 a pack of cards

Each player takes a card. The player with the highest card is the dictator. The dictator then announces some card-based condition(s) and deals out up to five cards per player. For every card a player has that meets the announced conditions, they have a drink. The dictator is also dealt a hand of cards, except nominating, rather than taking, a drink. After dealing, the dictatorship passes to the left.

Example conditions: all even cards, all spades, all Aces etc.

The dictator can, of course, change the rules to whatever they want while they remain in power.

My Hat It Has Three Corners

Strength Rating –

You will need:

 drink

 friends

Sit in a circle. One person starts by singing:

'My hat it has three corners, Three corners has my hat,
And had it not three corners, It would not be my hat.'

44

Each person around the table follows suit. When it returns to the first person they remove the word 'hat', replace it with the action of pointing at your head, and everyone else repeats this. The game continues removing 'three' and replacing it with three fingers, and then removing 'corners' and replacing it with the action of turning a corner in a racing car (accompanied by the noise) respectively.

If you make a mistake you must have a drink.

Play Your Cards Wrong

Strength Rating –

You will need:

drink

friends

a pack of cards

Deal a card to a player. That player has to guess whether the next card will be higher or lower. If the guess is incorrect, the player must have a drink. If the guess was right, they get another go. If they survive for at least three cards they may choose to continue or to pass to the next player. When a player guesses wrongly, they must take a gulp of their drink for each card showing, therefore the idea is to build up as many cards as possible before passing it on to the next player.

If the next card is the same as the current card, this counts as a correct guess.

Kipper Racing

Strength Rating –

You will need:

 drink

 friends

 newspaper

 a pair of scissors

 some magazines

Cut the shape of a kipper from the newspaper for each player. Place the 'kippers' on the floor in a row. Each player stands behind their own kipper, and must flap it to the finish line using a magazine. The last one to get their kipper to the finish line in each game must have some of their drink.

Coin Football

Strength Rating –

You will need:

 drink

 friends

 3 coins

Two players at a time sit at either end of a wooden table. One player uses the fingers of their left hand to create a 'goal', while the other player uses one finger to shove the three coins across part of the table towards the goal. They must then select one coin, and try to shove it between the two others, and again shove a coin through the two others until they get a shot at the goal with one of the coins.

If they score, the other player must have some of their drink. If they are unable to flick a coin between the other two, play swaps to the other person who puts the three coins together and launches a counter attack. The loser of each goal must have a drink. If more than two players are present, the winner stays in their seat while someone replaces the loser in each game.

Bluffer!

Strength Rating –

You will need:

 drink

 up to 6 people

a pack of cards

The object of this game is to get rid of all your cards. Sit in a circle, deal the cards evenly, and take it in turns to lay face down your Aces, then your twos, etc. If a player doesn't have any of that sort of card, they must lie.

52

If someone thinks they are lying, they say 'Bluffer!' If that person is right, the bluffer takes a number of gulps of their drink proportional to the number of cards in the stack. If someone is wrongly accused of bluffing, the accuser must drink the prescribed amount. Whenever someone has drunk the number of gulps equating to the number of cards in the stack, they must then pick up all the cards in that stack and add them to their own. The winner is the first to run out of cards.

Entwined

Strength Rating –

You will need:

 drink

 3-6 friends

 a pack of cards

Deal out the cards to the players in a clockwise direction, face down. Each player must keep their hand out of sight of the other players.

The player to the left of the dealer starts by laying down one of their cards, face

54

up. The other players in turn must each lay down a card of the same face value. When the play gets to someone who does not have a card of the same face value, that player becomes 'entwined' and must have a drink. The next player may then play any card. If the 'entwined' player doesn't have that card either they remain entwined, and must have another drink. Then plays shifts back to the other player adjacent to the entwined player. This person then plays any card. This goes back and forth until the 'entwined' player gets released by playing the same face value card as one of the adjacent players.

Play continues until a player plays their last card. Once this happens, the rest of the players must count their remaining cards and take that number of gulps of their drink.

Animal, Vegetable or Mineral . . .

Strength Rating –

You will need:

 drink

 friends

Take it in turns to think of an object that fits one of the animal, vegetable or mineral categories. The other players have three questions each, to which the person being questioned must answer 'yes' or 'no'. (The first question should

56

always be, 'Are you animal, vegetable or mineral?')

If a player fails to guess correctly within three questions they must drink and the questioning moves to the next person. If a player's three questions are all answered 'yes', but without leading to a final identification, that player may continue to ask questions until they receive a 'no' or until they correctly identify the animal, vegetable or mineral.

The Flicks

Strength Rating – 🍺🍺🍺

You will need:

 drink

friends

 a coin

an empty glass

The object of this game is not to win or lose, merely to keep in the game. Essentially, all you have to do is to bounce a coin on its flat side into the empty glass. Each player takes a turn at doing this, and when anyone succeeds they can nominate another person to take a gulp of their drink. They must continue to take flicks of the coin until they miss. When a player misses, they can have another attempt if they want, but a second failure is punished by drinking themselves.

When a player has scored three consecutive successful shots, they can nominate every other player to drink two times the agreed amount each.

Queens

Strength Rating –

You will need:

 drink

 friends

 a pack of cards

Shuffle the cards, then spread them out on the table so that any can be chosen. Take it in turns to pick a card at random, then perform the following duties according to the cards picked:

Ace = Choose any player to drink

King = All players drink

Queen = Women drink

Jack = Men drink

10 = 2nd person on right of chooser must drink

9 = 2nd person on left of chooser drinks

8 = All players drink

7 = Person to right of chooser drinks

6 = Person to left of chooser drinks

5 = Change direction of play

4 to 1 = The person picking the card must take that number of gulps of their drink

Fifty-Fifty

Strength Rating –

You will need:

 drink

 friends

 a beer mat

This is the simplest game *on the planet*, and therefore highly recommended for those who feel they are *off it*.

Take a beer mat, and flip it into the air. If it lands face up, nominate someone to have some of their drink. If it lands face down, you have to drink. Each person takes it in turns to flip the mat, with a fifty-fifty chance of either having to have a drink or nominate one to someone else.

The game works best if people conspire to nominate just one person to have a drink whenever they win.

Harry

Strength Rating –

You will need:

 drink

 friends

Players need to sit in a circle or around a table. The game starts by one player looking at another player and saying 'Harry?' The second person must respond by saying 'Yes Harry?' to the first person, who then says 'Tell Harry'. That concludes the first round.

The next stage is for the second person to say 'Harry' to third member of the group, who must then respond by saying 'Yes Harry?' to the second player and in turn they must say it to the first player. The first player who started the game again says 'Tell Harry'. Simple really!

If a player slips up or hesitates they must have a drink and they are then known as 'Harry One Spot'.

WHO IS THIS HARRY ANYWAY?!!

Card Head

Strength Rating –

You will need:

 drink

 friends

 a pack of cards

Players sit in a circle. Each player is dealt a card which they have to stick on their forehead without looking at it. If you can't get the card to stay on your head hold it on with your finger.

You'll be able to see the value of your fellow players' cards but you won't have any idea of what your own card is.

The idea is to gamble as to whether you think your own card is higher than that of your friends. If you take a bet and lose, you must have a drink.

Cheers

Strength Rating –

You will need:

 drink

 friends

The game starts when the first person lifts their glass to toast something of their preference, such as 'Cheers to the fine weather!' Everybody knocks their glasses together and takes two drinks from their glass.

The toasts continue around the table as fast as possible, with each person saying their personal 'cheers to . . .' and drinking two gulps of their drink each time.

This is a very merry game but it can get quite loud due to the knocking together of glasses and rowdy toasting. You'll probably find that the volume increases as the toast tally rises!

Sardines

Strength Rating –

You will need:

 drink

 friends

 somewhere to hide

One person takes a full glass of drink and hides with it somewhere in the building or grounds. The others must try to find them. When someone finds them, they must have a drink from their glass, and the other person now hides

70

with them. When someone finds them both, they must both drink from their glasses, and all three people now hide.

The last person to find the hidden people must take a number of gulps of their drink equal to the number of people in the hiding place.

International Drinking Rules

Strength Rating –

You will need:

drink

friends

These are the rules:

1. No pointing (you can use your elbows to gesture).
2. No swearing.

72

3. You must drink with the hand that you don't normally use (e.g. your left if you are right-handed) and with your little finger pointing out.

If you break the rules you must have a drink.

This is a copy-cat game, but instead of a 'Simon says . . .' instruction, the players must deduce by observation the action they must copy. Any player may choose to do an action at any time. For example; someone might decide to put their thumb on their forehead, and everyone has to follow suit. The last person to catch on has to have a drink.

Happy Shopper

Strength Rating –

You will need:

 drink

 friends

 pen and paper

 plastic shopping bags

 a watch

Make a list of 5 household items; a piece of toilet paper, a plaster, a fork etc, making sure that there will be enough of each to go round (there's no point in writing 'a tin of cat food' down on the list if you only have one!). Nominate one person to be the referee. Each of the 'shoppers' must have a plastic shopping bag. The referee stands at 'base' (e.g. the living room). When the referee says 'Go!' the players have five minutes in which to find all the items on the list and return home with them to base. The last person back must down an entire glass of their drink. Play continues with a new list and referee.

The Orange Game

Strength Rating –

You will need:

 drink

 friends

 an orange

All players stand in a line, and the first one places the orange under their chin. Each player must pass the orange along the line from person to person without using their hands.

The Tackle Game

Strength Rating –

You will need:

 drink

 friends

 a television

Players must divide themselves into two teams, and sit around a television watching a contact sport, such as football or rugby. Each team on the sofa will identify with one on the television.

Whenever someone from your team makes a tackle, all members of the other team must have a drink. If a goal or a try is scored, the losing team must drink two times the agreed amount each.

Racing Demon

Strength Rating –

You will need:

 drink

 friends

 a die

 a selection of old clothes
(scarf, coat, gloves, pair of
trousers etc)

Sit in a circle. Place the clothes and a glass of booze in the centre. Each player takes it in turn to throw the die. When a player throws a six they must run to the centre of the circle, put on the clothes and drink from the centre glass. They must continue drinking until another player throws a six and replaces them.

This can be quite a rowdy one - and you'll probably need to top up the centre glass from time to time!

Guess the Ad

Strength Rating –

You will need:

     drink

     friends

     a television

Put the television on and wait for the adverts to come up.

Take it in turns to guess what each advert is for, within five seconds of it starting. If a player gets it wrong they must have a drink. Player two gets the second advert, player three the third, etc.

Usually there will be sufficient adverts for up to five or six people, with opportunities to play coming up every fifteen minutes.

The Dealer and the Fuzz

Strength Rating –

You will need:

 drink

 friends

 one playing card per person – within these, one King and one Ace

Players must sit in a circle. The cards are then dealt face down. Everyone takes a quick look at theirs. The person who gets the King is *the fuzz* and the person who gets the Ace is the *dealer*. The dealer must very discreetly wink at one of the other players, who will eventually say, 'the deal has been made'. At this time the fuzz identifies themself and tries to guess who the dealer is. If the fuzz chooses the wrong player they must have a drink. If they choose wrong again, they must drink the number on the wrongly accused person's card, for example, ten gulps for a ten of clubs. When the fuzz finally chooses correctly, the dealer has to drink the total number on the remaining cards. After this, the cards are shuffled, re-dealt and the game continues.

Gargle-Gurgle

Strength Rating –

You will need:

 drink

 friends

A slightly messier version of *Name That Tune*. Each player takes it in turns to perform a song for their 'audience'. The catch is that songs cannot be sung - they must be gargled! The other players take turns to identify the song, and an

86

incorrect guess is punished by a drinking penalty.

If, after a second gargled rendition, none of the players can guess the tune, the performer must finish an agreed quantity of their drink.

One Brown Hen

Strength Rating –

You will need:

drink

friends

The first person starts by saying 'one brown hen'. This is repeated around the table. The first person then adds 'one brown hen and a couple of ducks' and the phrase continues round. After this, the phrases accumulate in the order below. Any mistakes are punished by drinking.

Phrases:

- 3 running hares

- 4 brown bears

- 5 fat females fisting for a fight

- 6 Sicilian seamen sailing the seven seas

- 7 swans swimming on a shimmering lake

- 8 eager eagles eating Easter eggs

- 9 nuns knocking on the sacred door

- 10 tenors tunefully playing the tambourine

Darts

Strength Rating –

You will need:

 drink

 friends

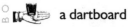 a dartboard

Each player throws three darts, and must drink according to the following scores:

1 - 20	= 4 gulps
21 - 30	= 3 gulps
31 - 40	= 2 gulps
41 - 50	= 1 gulp
51 or more	= no penalty

Twenty-One

Strength Rating –

You will need:

 drink

 friends

 a pack of cards

The object of the game is to get as close to 21 points in your hand without going over. Aces are 11, all face cards are 10 points, and all other cards are face value.

Deal two cards to each player, one face-down, and one face-up. The play rotates, like in Pontoon, for additional cards ('twist'). If you think you have a high hand, 18 points or so, you can 'knock', which means everyone else has to take one more card. After everyone has taken their last card, the hands are laid down and the person with the lowest point total has to have a drink. If the person who knocked has the lowest point total, that player must also drink an additional penalty for poor play. If a player gets more than 21, they must have a drink. If someone has a precise total of 21 in their hand, they immediately place their cards down and everyone else must drink.

ALSO FROM SUMMERSDALE

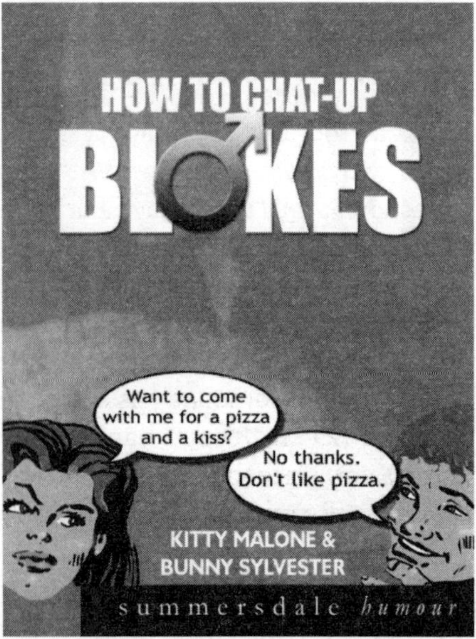

www.summersdale.com